Patriotic Songs

You're a Grand Old Flag

A Jubilant Song About Old Glory

Written by George M. Cohan
Edited by Ann Owen • Illustrated by Todd Ouren

Music Adviser: Peter Mercer-Taylor, Ph.D.
Associate Professor of Musicology, University of Minnesota, Minneapolis

Reading Adviser: Susan Kesselring, M.A., Literacy Educator
Rosemount-Apple Valley-Eagan (Minnesota) School District

PICTURE WINDOW BOOKS
Minneapolis, Minnesota

Patriotic Songs series editor: Sara E. Hoffmann
Musical arrangement: Elizabeth Temple
Designer: John Moldstad
Page production: Picture Window Books
The illustrations in this book were prepared digitally.

Printed in the United States of America.

Picture Window Books
5115 Excelsior Boulevard
Suite 232
Minneapolis, MN 55416
1-877-845-8392
www.picturewindowbooks.com

Library of Congress Cataloging-in-Publication Data
Cohan, George M. (George Michael), 1878-1942. You're a grand
old flag / by George M. Cohan ; edited by Ann Owen ; illustrated by Todd Ouren.
p. cm. — (Patriotic songs)
Summary: Presents the complete text of this patriotic song that was written for a
Broadway musical, chronicles the history of the American flag, and recounts the life of
the song's composer, George M. Cohan. Includes instructions for making a flag wind
sock.
ISBN 1-4048-0173-1
1. Patriotic music—United States—History and criticism—Juvenile literature. 2. Flags—
United States—Juvenile literature. 3. Cohan, George M. (George Michael), 1878-1942—
Juvenile literature. [1. Patriotic music. 2. Songs. 3. Flags—United States—History.
4. Cohan, George M. (George Michael), 1878-1942.] I. Owen, Ann, 1953-
II. Ouren, Todd, ill. III. Title. IV. Series.
ML3551.C56 2003
782.42'1599'0973—dc21
                                                            2002155015

O say, can you hear America singing?

America's patriotic songs are a record of the country's history.

Many of these songs were written when the United States was young.

Some songs were inspired by war and some by thoughts of peace and freedom.

They all reflect the country's spirit and dreams.

Forever in peace may you wave

You're a grand old flag,
you're a high-flying flag,

and forever in peace may you wave.

You're the emblem of the land I love,

the home of the free and the brave.

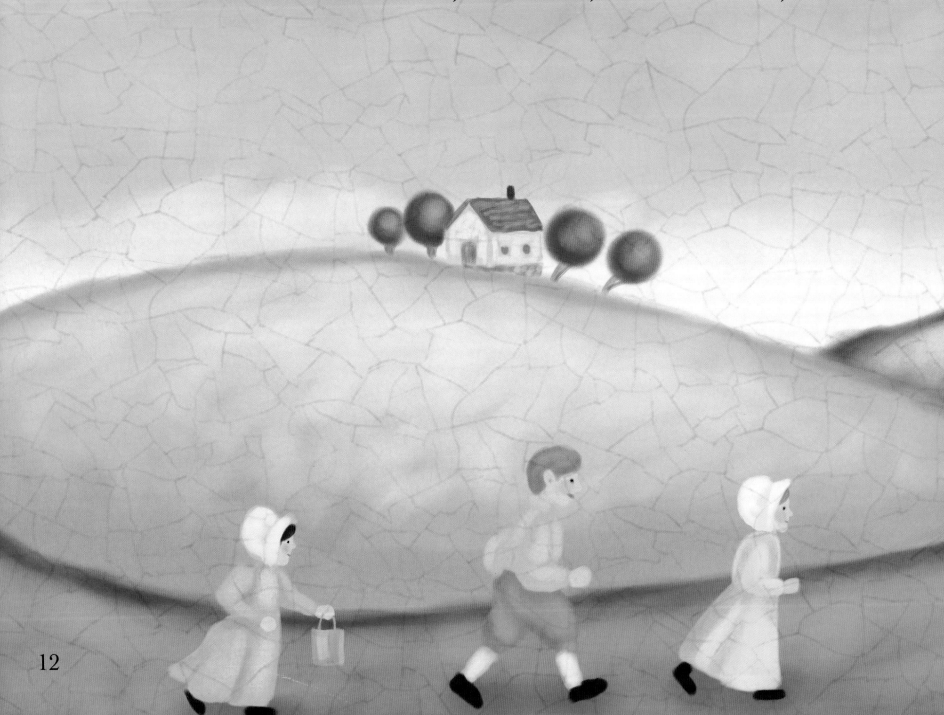

Ev'ry heart beats true
'neath the Red, White, and Blue,

where there's never a boast or a brag.

Should auld acquaintance be forgot,

keep your eye on the grand old flag.

The United States has had many "Grand Old Flags." While all of them have used the familiar colors and stars and stripes, no two have looked exactly alike. In 1777, the Continental Congress passed the first flag act: "Resolved, That the flag of the United States be made of thirteen stripes, alternate red and white; that the union be thirteen stars, white in a blue field, representing a new Constellation." The Flag Act of 1818 provided for 13 stripes and one star for each state. The flag kept changing as new states joined the country. We have had our current flag since 1960, after Hawaii entered the nation.

You're a Grand Old Flag

You're a grand old flag, you're a high-fly-ing flag, and for-ev-er in peace may you wave. You're the em-blem of the land I love, the home of__ the free and__ the brave. Ev'-ry heart beats true 'neath the Red, White, and Blue, where there's nev-er a boast or a brag. Should auld ac-quain-tance be for-got, keep your eye on__ the grand old flag.

There's a feeling comes a-stealing,
And it sets my brain a-reeling,
When I'm listening to the music of a military band.
Any tune like "Yankee Doodle"
Simply sets me off my noodle.
It's that patriotic something that no one can understand.

"Way down south, in the land of cotton"—
Melody untiring, ain't that inspiring?
Hurrah! Hurrah! We'll join the Jubilee!
And that's going some for the Yankees, by gum!
Red, White, and Blue, I am for you!
Honest, you're a grand old flag!

About the Song

"You're a Grand Old Flag" was written by George M. Cohan in 1906. He wrote it for his play *George Washington, Jr.* The idea for the song came to him after he met a man who fought in the Civil War. The man carried the flag during the battle of Gettysburg.

George wrote the music and words for 40 musicals, or plays that have songs in them. He also usually directed, produced, and starred in the musicals. Most people think George started musical comedy theater.

George liked to write plays and songs about patriotism. Few people today know his plays, but many of his songs are still popular. Besides "You're a Grand Old Flag," two other well-known patriotic songs he wrote are "Yankee Doodle Dandy" and "Over There."

"Over There" was written on April 7, 1917, the day after the United States entered World War I. Many people think of it as the most popular patriotic American war song. In 1941, President Franklin Roosevelt gave the Congressional Medal of Honor to George. The president said the honor was "in belated recognition of the authorship of 'Over There.'"

You Can Make a Grand Old Stars and Stripes Wind Sock

What you need:

Blue and white construction paper

Scissors

A round box (such as an oatmeal box or potato chip tube)

Glue and tape

White and red paper streamers

Hole punch

String

An adult to help you

What to do:

1. Trace or draw stars on the white construction paper.
2. Cut out the stars.
3. Ask an adult to help you cut the bottom off the box so it is open at both ends.
4. Wrap blue construction paper around the box and tape or glue it in place.
5. Glue the white stars onto the blue background. Cut some white and red streamers and tape them to one end of the box.
6. Punch four holes around the edge of the other end of the box. The holes should be spread evenly around the edge.
7. Cut two pieces of string, each about 18 inches (.5 m) long. Tie the ends of the strings to the box, one end for each hole.
8. Cut a longer piece of string. This is the string you will use for hanging the wind sock, so make it as long as you need. Tie one end of this string to the smaller pieces.
9. Your wind sock is ready to hang and wave.

To Learn More

At the Library
Binns, Tristan Boyer. *The American Flag*. Chicago: Heinemann Library, 2001.

Kroll, Steven. *By the Dawn's Early Light: The Story of the Star-Spangled Banner*. New York: Scholastic, 1994.

Krull, Kathleen. *Gonna Sing My Head Off!: American Folk Songs for Children*. New York: A. A. Knopf, 1992.

Raatma, Lucia. *Patriotism*. Mankato, Minn.: Bridgestone Books, 2000.

Ryan, Pam Muñoz. *The Flag We Love*. Watertown, Mass.: Charlesbridge Pub., 1996.

On the Web
FirstGov for Kids
http://www.kids.gov
For fun links and information about the United States and its government

National Institute of Environmental Health Sciences Kids' Page: Patriotic Songs
http://www.niehs.nih.gov/kids/musicpatriot.htm
For lyrics and music to your favorite patriotic songs

Want to learn more about patriotic songs?
Visit FACT HOUND at http://www.facthound.com.